Original title:
The Secret Beyond

Copyright © 2024 Creative Arts Management OÜ
All rights reserved.

Author: Harris Montgomery
ISBN HARDBACK: 978-9916-88-976-3
ISBN PAPERBACK: 978-9916-88-977-0

Tides of the Concealed Truth

Waves crest secrets on the shore,
Echoes whisper tales of yore.
Beneath the calm, the currents flow,
What lies beneath, we may not know.

Moonlit paths of silver thread,
Guide the lost where few have tread.
Tides pull at the heart's embrace,
Revealing truths we dare not face.

Imaginary Flora of the Dreamscape

Petals bloom in hues of night,
Colors dance in soft moonlight.
Thoughts like vines entwine our mind,
In this realm, all dreams unwind.

Whispers of a distant song,
Guiding us where we belong.
In gardens rich with fleeting grace,
Each flower smiles, a warm embrace.

The Light That Never Was

Flickers fade in the twilight,
Casting shadows, chasing light.
Illusions forged in empty space,
A ghostly glow we can't embrace.

Memories painted in pale hues,
Drifting softly like morning dew.
What was real now slips away,
In the silence, we long to stay.

Paths to the Mysterious Interlude

Winding roads of mist and haze,
Lead us through a fleeting maze.
Footsteps soft on ancient stone,
In each echo, we're not alone.

Branches stretch like guiding hands,
Through the mist, a shadow stands.
Pause and breathe, the world is still,
In this moment, time can thrill.

Threads of Reality Yet to Be Discovered

In the twilight of dreams, we weave,
Invisible strands of hope and light.
Each moment whispers, daring to believe,
A tapestry forming through the night.

In corners unseen, truths may lie,
Watched by the stars that softly gleam.
With every heartbeat, we reach for the sky,
In the fabric of fate, we chase a dream.

Threads of wonder, both fragile and bold,
Intertwined stories, yet to unfold.
With every choice, new paths will bend,
In the dance of time, all fates blend.

Through the mists of doubt, we will roam,
Discovering worlds where shadows play.
In the heart of chaos, we find our home,
Threads of reality guide our way.

Patterns in the Fabric of Shadows

Shadows whisper secrets we can't see,
Mapping patterns in the fading light.
They dance on walls, wild and free,
A story woven from day to night.

In the silence, a rhythm beats,
Echoes linger, secrets unfold.
In whispered tales, the light retreats,
The fabric of shadows, silent and bold.

Each silhouette holds a tale to tell,
Where dreams collide with fears we keep.
In hidden corners, we know them well,
The patterns weave while the world sleeps.

Through the darkness, the truth emerges,
In every fold, a mystery waits.
We search for meaning as the night surges,
In shadows' embrace, we navigate fates.

Whispers of Hidden Realms

Beneath the surface, worlds await,
Where echoes linger in forgotten halls.
Whispers beckon, tempting fate,
In hidden realms, the silence calls.

Secrets float on the evening breeze,
Carried softly from distant lands.
In tangled woods or swaying trees,
A magic pulses, threaded strands.

Visions flicker in twilight's glow,
Revealing paths we cannot see.
In the quiet, our hearts will sow,
The seeds of dreams, yearning to be free.

Listen closely, the call is clear,
For within the shadows, truth does swell.
In hidden realms, we conquer fear,
With every whisper, we weave our spell.

Echoes from the Unknown

In the depths of silence, echoes ring,
Haunting notes from realms afar.
Voices linger, a haunting swing,
Connecting us to the cosmic star.

Each sound a memory, faint and sweet,
Resonating through the veil of time.
In the patterns, fate and chance meet,
Trembling echoes in rhythm and rhyme.

Through darkness crept, a light breaks through,
Unraveling stories shrouded in gray.
In every echo, a glimpse of the true,
Whispers of worlds that lead the way.

From the unknown, tales emerge clear,
In the dance of shadows, we find our grace.
With every heartbeat, we hold them near,
Echoes from the unknown, our sacred space.

Beyond the Mask

In shadows where the silence dwells,
A hidden truth that softly swells.
Behind the grin, a world unseen,
A fractured soul, a restless dream.

The echoes dance in muted light,
A whispered tale of grief and might.
Each mask a story, worn with pride,
Yet deep within, the fears confide.

Each gaze a question, broad and wide,
What lies beneath, what do we hide?
The laughter rings, yet tears may flow,
In every smile, a thread of woe.

Beyond the mask, the heart can speak,
In silent moments, deep and bleak.
For every face that greets the day,
A thousand secrets lost at play.

Fables of the Unimagined

In realms where dreams take root and fly,
A canvas wide beneath the sky.
Fables weave through twilight's hue,
Myths awaken, ancient and new.

Underneath a silver gleam,
Wonders born from thought's wild stream.
Whispered tales that softly call,
In moonlit realms we chase them all.

Creatures dance on starlit paths,
Offering joy and secret laughs.
In every story, worlds collide,
In fables vast, we seek to guide.

Embrace the quirky, strange, and rare,
For in the unimagined, we dare.
To find the truth in fancied lore,
Unlocking hearts forevermore.

Secrets Cradled in Time

Beneath the surface, shadows sigh,
Time wraps secrets, silent, nigh.
Echoes of laughter, whispers lost,
In every moment, hidden cost.

Old trees hold tales in twisted roots,
While winds recall forgotten flutes.
Cradled softly, the years they keep,
In muted dreams, the past will sleep.

Ancient stones, a witness to lore,
Each crack and crevice holds much more.
A tapestry of lives once spun,
Behind closed doors, life's race is run.

In silence woven, history sways,
Secrets unraveled in twilight's haze.
Each heartbeat echoes through the chime,
Unlocking magic, cradled in time.

Lurking Wonders

Beneath the surface, shadows creep,
In stillness, wonders carefully sleep.
Whispers brush against the night,
Lurking dreams take graceful flight.

In every corner, tales reside,
Mysteries wrapped, like secrets bide.
A gentle breeze, a fleeting glance,
Invites us to a hidden dance.

Stars align with stories grand,
Galaxies formed by a fragile hand.
In darkened nooks, where echoes play,
Lurking wonders softly sway.

Journey forth and dare to find,
The hidden treasures, intertwined.
For life conceals both joy and strife,
In lurking wonders, the essence of life.

Portraits of the Unknown

In shadows of hushed twilight,
Faces of dreams reside.
They beckon with soft whispers,
A tale of worlds untied.

Each gaze holds a secret,
A journey untraveled yet.
With stories left unspoken,
In memories we forget.

Brush strokes of the unseen,
Palette of the lost past.
A canvas of silent voices,
Where echoes everlast.

The unknown calls us gently,
To dance in the gray dawn.
Through windows of imagination,
In the silence, we are drawn.

Insights from the Wisteria Grove

Amidst the lilac blossoms,
Time seems to stand still.
Whispers of the gentle breeze,
Echo secrets of the hill.

Sunlight filters through branches,
A soft, dappled light.
Petals flutter like laughter,
In this realm of pure delight.

Each root holds deep stories,
Of love and loss entwined.
The wisteria wraps around,
Healing hearts that once pined.

Moments captured in fragrance,
A heartstrings' tender pull.
In this grove of wisdom,
Our spirits find their lull.

Beyond the Echoing Chamber

In chambers wide and empty,
Voices linger in the air.
Thoughts bounce off the silence,
Each echo laid bare.

Shadows dance along walls,
Memories weave their tale.
Yet hope finds a footing,
In the heart, we prevail.

Walls that once felt confining,
Now inspire new dreams.
Through whispers of the past,
The future brightly beams.

Beyond the echoing chamber,
New breath of life is drawn.
In this vastness we wander,
Towards the transforming dawn.

The Lurking Whisper of the Void

A darkness not unkind,
Stirs softly in the night.
The void calls out in silence,
With echoes of lost light.

An unseen hand reaches forth,
To brush against the soul.
In the depths of uncertainty,
We find what makes us whole.

Each shadow holds a secret,
In the fabric of the dark.
The whisper speaks of freedom,
In the stillness, we embark.

The void, a canvas waiting,
For colors to emerge.
In the lurking, we find purpose,
As our spirits gently surge.

Secrets Beneath the Surface

Whispers float in tranquil streams,
Beneath the calm, a world redeems.
Hidden tales in silken tides,
Unraveled truths our heart abides.

Waves conceal what shadows crave,
Secrets woven, bold and brave.
Stories lost and gently kept,
In watery depths, where dreams have slept.

Fingers trace the fleeting flow,
Echoed songs from long ago.
In silence, wisdom doth abide,
Unseen layers where we confide.

Bubbles rise with every sigh,
Underneath the vast, blue sky.
What lies beneath may burst our seams,
Unlock the world of whispered dreams.

Lurking in the Abyss

In shadows deep, a silence sprawls,
An echoing void within its walls.
Darkness holds its breath in thrall,
Deep secrets wait for fate's own call.

Beneath the waves, the phantoms creep,
Invisible, where sorrows weep.
Thoughts entwined in webs of night,
Haunted dreams just out of sight.

A flicker stirs among the gloom,
Rippling fears begin to loom.
In the quiet, truths reside,
In the void's embrace, they hide.

Monsters form of whispered dread,
Half-formed visions in our head.
What we seek may not return,
In the abyss, we live and learn.

The Unseen Journey

Paths unknown weave through the mist,
An unseen journey, a silent twist.
Footsteps echo on untouched ground,
In every choice, new worlds are found.

Stars aligned yet far from view,
Guiding hearts to what is true.
With every turn, a shadow grows,
In the dark, our courage flows.

Moments fleeting, time suspended,
Every heartbeat, a tale extended.
In the whispers of the breeze,
The journey lives, infused with ease.

Landmarks fade, but dreams ignite,
Through every struggle, we find our light.
What lies ahead, a question marked,
In this unseen path, embers sparked.

Silhouettes of Illusion

Shapes of black against the light,
Figures dance with ghostly might.
Fleeting forms in shadows play,
Haunting echoes of yesterday.

Veils of mist conceal the truth,
Chasing phantoms of lost youth.
In the twilight, visions blend,
Where beginnings meet the end.

Glimmers tease the eye's delight,
In the dark, they take to flight.
What we see may not be real,
In silhouettes, the heart can feel.

Beneath the surface, dreams unfold,
Trading secrets, traded gold.
In this gallery of the mind,
Illusions linger, love entwined.

Whispers of the Hidden Path

In twilight's soft embrace we tread,
Beneath the ancient trees we wed.
The murmurs of the forest call,
With secrets in their whispers small.

A path entwined with shadows deep,
Where every silence seems to weep.
The air thick with a magic rare,
Invites the wanderers to dare.

A flicker lights the way ahead,
In valleys where the dreams are shed.
With every step, a tale unfolds,
Of journeys past and futures bold.

So let the whispers guide you near,
Embrace the path, release your fear.
For in the hidden thickets lie,
The echoes of a silent sigh.

Echoes of the Unseen Journey

In shadows cast by moonlit glow,
We walk where silent waters flow.
Each ripple holds a story lost,
Of every heart that paid the cost.

The echoes in the stillness speak,
Of paths once tread by those who seek.
Where footprints fade like misty dreams,
And nothing is exactly as it seems.

The world outside is bright and loud,
Yet here we stand beneath the cloud.
For every step upon this ground,
The pulse of time is all around.

So listen close, let spirits guide,
Through unseen realms, we'll slip and slide.
In echoes of the journey bold,
The unseen truths begin to unfold.

Veils of the Forgotten Realm

Beneath the surface, worlds collide,
Where veils of mist and dreams abide.
In hidden corners, shadows loom,
And silence births a whispered tune.

The tale of time in ruins told,
Of pasts adorned in silver and gold.
In searching eyes, the mysteries gleam,
A forgotten realm, a half-remembered dream.

With every sigh, the veil grows thin,
Unraveling threads where we begin.
The tapestry of fates entwined,
In shadows cast by thoughts confined.

So venture forth with heart in hand,
To realms where echoes softly stand.
In veils of stories left to hide,
The forgotten truth seeks to abide.

In Search of Shadowed Truths

Through tangled paths where secrets lie,
I chase the shadows passing by.
With every whisper, I draw near,
To truths obscured but ever clear.

Beneath the stars, the night unfolds,
In quiet dance, the story molds.
Each step I take reveals the grace,
Of hidden dreams in hidden space.

The flicker of the candle light,
Guides me gently through the night.
In search of truths that dare not show,
I weave through shadows, soft and slow.

Embrace the darkness, hold it tight,
For in its depth, the heart takes flight.
In search of shadows, I create,
The stories that my soul will sate.

Remnants of Forgotten Dreams

In shadows linger hopes of old,
Silent whispers, tales untold.
Fragmented visions start to fade,
Memories of what we once made.

Time erases, but we still yearn,
For flickers of a fire that burns.
Lost in the echo of a sigh,
Dreams twist like smoke in the sky.

Pieces scattered through the mist,
Promises we thought we'd kissed.
Yet in the silence, sparks remain,
Remnants of joy mingled with pain.

Awaken now from slumber deep,
Embrace the dreams that dare to leap.
Though faded, they can still ignite,
A guiding star through the night.

Enquire Within

Within the silence, secrets hide,
Whispers echo, hearts collide.
Questions linger, answers stray,
Truth awaits, don't turn away.

In the mirror, gaze a while,
Search the depths, uncover the smile.
Layers peel, the soul's revealed,
In quietude, wounds can be healed.

Listen closely, hear your voice,
In every choice, rejoice, rejoice.
The journey turns, the path unwinds,
All you seek is in your mind.

Amidst the chaos, find the calm,
Nurture the heart, provide the balm.
Inquire deeply, let love flow,
The light within will help you grow.

The Whispering Woods

Beneath the boughs where shadows creep,
Ancient secrets lull and keep.
Branches sway with tales of yore,
Nature sings, forevermore.

As twilight drapes its velvet shroud,
The forest breathes, alive and proud.
Echoes dance on a gentle breeze,
Rustling leaves, a soft tease.

Creatures stir in the fading light,
Guided by the moon's soft bite.
Footsteps tread on a hidden trail,
In this realm, we shall not fail.

Listen close to the soft refrain,
The whispering woods call our name.
In every rustle, every sigh,
A magic lingers, drawing nigh.

Canvases of Deception

Brush strokes hide the darkest fears,
Painted smiles mask silent tears.
Colors clash, a vibrant guise,
Artful lies, crafted alibis.

Layers built on fragile dreams,
Perceptions shaped by silver beams.
What is real? Where's the truth?
In shadows dwell the whispers of youth.

Frames encase a world askew,
Beauty trapped, we misconstrue.
Behind the glass, the heart lay bare,
Longing glances, a wistful stare.

Revealed in strokes, a story spins,
Canvases where deception begins.
In every painting, life reflects,
The art of truth, it disconnects.

Tales from the Edge of Night

In the shadows where whispers dwell,
Moonlight weaves a secret spell.
Stars murmur tales of dreams long lost,
In the silence, we count the cost.

The breeze carries a ghostly sound,
As night unfolds its velvet ground.
Footsteps echo on cobblestone,
In the dark, we are not alone.

Flickering lamps, a guiding light,
Cast away shadows, embrace the night.
Stories linger in the cool air,
Every heartbeat, a lingering prayer.

Embrace the dark, let visions soar,
For each ending opens a door.
In the edge of night, we find our way,
Tales woven in the light of day.

Chronicles of the Unexplored

Beyond the veil where dreams reside,
Lies a world where wonders hide.
Paths untraveled call our name,
In the wild, nothing's the same.

Mountains whisper ancient lore,
Rivers sing of times before.
Every step on unmarked ground,
A treasure trove yet to be found.

The sky unfolds in hues so bold,
Promises of stories yet untold.
With every heartbeat, we ignite,
The chronicles of the unexplored night.

In shadows deep, we seek the light,
Wandering souls in endless flight.
Together we chart the unknown,
In the heart of the earth, we find our home.

Hints from the Echoing Silence

In the stillness, whispers bloom,
Secrets linger, weaving gloom.
Silent shadows dance and sway,
Hints of truth softly betray.

Among the echoes, hope takes flight,
Carried gently by the night.
Gentle sighs and fleeting dreams,
In silence, nothing's as it seems.

The heart listens, tuned to the sound,
In the quiet, wisdom is found.
Between each breath, a story flows,
Hints of silence nobody knows.

With every pause, a world unfolds,
The language of silence breaks the molds.
In the echoes, we learn to hear,
The magic that lingers, ever near.

The Hidden Orchestra of Existence

In the heartbeat of the earth, we find,
A symphony, beautifully entwined.
Each leaf rustles, a note so sweet,
Nature's rhythm, a pulsing beat.

Waves crash softly upon the shore,
Whispers of secrets, life's endless score.
The wind carries songs from afar,
Every creature, a shining star.

In the dawn's light, the chorus grows,
Colors dance, the melody flows.
Life awakens, an endless song,
In this orchestra, we all belong.

As twilight wraps the world in grace,
Harmony blooms in every space.
In this union, we find our part,
The hidden orchestra sings from the heart.

Fascination with the Invisible

In shadows where the stillness breathes,
Lies the dance of wonders unseen.
The whispers of thoughts and dreams weave,
Creating worlds where hearts convene.

Like starlight dimmed by quiet night,
Secrets float in the deep air.
Glimmers of truth shed gentle light,
Invisible threads, beyond compare.

Each heartbeat pulses with pure grace,
In realms where silence paints the scene.
We yearn to touch, to sense, embrace,
The essence of what might have been.

Through veils of time, we search and seek,
For magic spooled in every sigh.
The unseen speaks, though soft and meek,
In fascination, we learn to fly.

The Chasm of Enchantment

Beyond the edge where shadows fall,
A chasm wide, a leap of faith.
In depths of night, we hear the call,
A haunting tune, a whispered wraith.

The stars ignite the velvet void,
Lost echoes dance in spectral light.
In dreams we weave, our hearts overjoyed,
Across the chasm, we take flight.

With every step, the world dissolves,
In colors bright, our spirits soar.
The magic of it all evolves,
A symphony we can't ignore.

Embrace the fear, let go, transform,
In that abyss, our souls entwine.
For in the dark, new worlds are born,
Through enchantment, we shall align.

Traces of Whispers

In twilight's hush, the voices blend,
Echoes of time in tender space.
Each breath a link, a message penned,
In fading light, we find our place.

Like petals brushed by unseen hands,
The traces linger, soft and sweet.
Through sacred woods and shifting sands,
We follow where the echoes meet.

With every sigh, a story told,
In whispers soft, the night reveals.
The warmth of love, so deep, so bold,
In silent vows, the heart heals.

Each fleeting note of memory stirs,
Building bridges to the past.
In whispers, every longing blurs,
A tapestry of spells cast.

Heartbeats of the Unvoiced

In the stillness where silence reigns,
Heartbeats echo, soft and low.
Unvoiced dreams bear unseen chains,
Yet in their depth, the wishes grow.

Through labyrinths of hope and fear,
A rhythm pulses, raw and pure.
In every tear, a truth held dear,
The unvoiced yearn for love's allure.

Like shadows cast on winter's chill,
They dance beneath the surface bright.
Each heartbeat whispers, strong and still,
A promise bound by whispered light.

Together in the night we stand,
The heartbeats merge, a sacred trust.
In unity, we clasp our hands,
For unvoiced love will never rust.

Labyrinths of Uncertainty

In shadows deep, we walk the way,
Where paths twist and turn, night and day.
The whispers call, they lead us blind,
Through the maze of a restless mind.

Each choice a step, each step a chance,
Trapped in the echoes of fate's dance.
We wander, search for signs to see,
Yet truth eludes, like smoke in the lea.

Fears and dreams, they intertwine,
In corridors where hopes decline.
Yet still we search for light's embrace,
In the heart of this timeless space.

With every twist, we learn to cope,
In the labyrinths, we build our hope.
Though uncertainty reigns, we find our way,
In the night, we'll bloom at break of day.

Tales from Beyond the Veil

In the twilight, stories wake,
Whispers linger, softly quake.
Voices from the past draw near,
Tales of love, and tales of fear.

Ancient tales from shadowed nights,
Flickering flames, ghostly lights.
Echoes of those who've walked before,
Guide us through a spectral door.

Fables wrapped in time's embrace,
Each a glimpse of a lost face.
Secrets held in the still of night,
Unravel threads, bring words to light.

With every story, we connect,
Bridging realms with deep respect.
Beyond the veil, our hearts entwined,
In every tale, a truth defined.

Embrace of the Unknown

In the dark, where shadows play,
Dreams and fears begin to sway.
With every step, a pulse ignites,
   In the depth of starry nights.

We dance upon the edge of fate,
Embracing all that feels innate.
The thrill of wild, the chill of doubt,
In the unknown, we twist and shout.

Uncharted paths, they call our name,
   In each heartbeat, lies the flame.
Adventures wait in silent skies,
   In the uncertain, our spirit flies.

So take the leap, let courage show,
In the arms of what we don't know.
For in this journey, bold and bright,
We find our truth in the endless night.

The Hidden Tapestry

Thread by thread, secrets weave,
In every corner, whispers grieve.
Patterns dance in shadows cast,
Stories linger from the past.

Colors shift in twilight's glow,
Silken paths where dreams can flow.
Unraveling the veils of time,
Fragrant echoes, silent rhyme.

Each stitch holds a forgotten tale,
In wanderlust, the spirits sail.
Knots of fate entwined as one,
Underneath the mending sun.

Beneath the loom, the heart does sigh,
In tangled grace, the truths lie.
The tapestry, a world apart,
Holds the pulse of every heart.

Mystical Allure

In the moon's soft, silver light,
Mysteries blossom, pure and bright.
Whispers drift on winds unseen,
Enchanting realms where souls convene.

Stars collide in velvet skies,
Every twinkle holds a prize.
Glimmers of dreams, they call us near,
In unison, we drown our fear.

Waves of magic softly flow,
Guiding hearts where wild winds blow.
In the garden of the night,
Desires bloom in quiet flight.

Wrap me in your gentle charm,
Keep me safe from every harm.
In this dance of fate, we find,
The sacred bond that threads our mind.

The Silent Symphony

In quiet chambers, notes take flight,
Harmony wrapped in soft twilight.
Echoes whisper through the air,
In the silence, we find care.

Strings of fate vibrate and hum,
Every heartbeat, a subtle drum.
Melodies weave a tale divine,
In stillness, our souls align.

Rhythms pulse within the dark,
Each pause becomes a sacred mark.
Resonance flows through every vein,
In this calm, we shed our pain.

Together we compose the night,
In silence, we embrace the light.
A symphony of dreams untold,
In quiet whispers, love unfolds.

Thickets of Mystery

In tangled woods where shadows sigh,
Secrets linger, hidden high.
Branches weave a cryptic snare,
Nature guards what lies so rare.

Footsteps soft on mossy ground,
Echoes lost but never found.
Nature's whispers, soft and deep,
Guarding secrets, dark and steep.

Thickets twist like ancient dreams,
Veiling truths in flowing streams.
Paths unfold with each brave roam,
In the wild, we find our home.

Lost in layers, heartbeats race,
In dense embrace, we find our place.
Mysterious paths beckon near,
In the thickets, we hold dear.

Shimmering Reflections

In waters deep, where silence gleams,
Moonlight dances on silver streams.
Whispers echo on the breeze,
Secrets held among the trees.

Ripples shimmer with soft delight,
Guiding dreams through velvet night.
Each reflection tells a tale,
Of fleeting moments that prevail.

The stars above, a distant spark,
Illuminate the path, so dark.
In the stillness, wonders thrive,
Awakening the heart, alive.

Underneath the cloak of night,
Shimmering truths come into sight.
In tranquil pools, we find our way,
To embrace the dawn of a new day.

Beneath the Ephemeral

Amidst the petals, colors blend,
Fragile whispers, they ascend.
Life's sweet breath, a fleeting glow,
Moments pass, like soft, white snow.

Beneath the sky, both vast and wide,
Nature sings, with arms held wide.
Each heartbeat, a soft refrain,
In the dance of joy and pain.

Time flows like a gentle stream,
Holding close each precious dream.
In sunlight's kiss, we find the grace,
Of fleeting time we can embrace.

Gentle echoes of what was,
In every breath, a gentle buzz.
Beneath the ephemeral skies,
Beauty lingers, never dies.

The Dance of Secrecy

In twilight's veil, shadows play,
Secrets weave in a quiet way.
Whispers soft on a moonlit sea,
Dance of mystery, wild and free.

Feet gliding on the edge of night,
Stars hide deep, avoiding sight.
Masked in silence, the truth may lay,
In the gentle sway of dreams at bay.

With every turn, a hidden glance,
The heart beats fast in this dim dance.
What's concealed behind closed doors,
Glimmers softly, like distant shores.

Through veils of mist, we chase the light,
A waltz of secrets taking flight.
In the dance, both bold and shy,
The truth may whisper, never die.

Passage into the Unknowable

A path unfolds in the quiet shade,
Steps uncertain, yet unafraid.
Veils of time, shrouded ahead,
With every choice, a story spread.

The horizon calls, a beckoning light,
Guiding souls through the silent night.
Each step forward, a breath anew,
Into the wild, we find our view.

In shadows deep, we seek the truth,
Courage blooms, reclaiming youth.
A journey mapped by beating hearts,
In the unknown, each knowing starts.

So let us stride with spirits bold,
Into the mysteries yet untold.
For in this passage, we shall find,
The threads of fate, all intertwined.

Lights of Unfathomed Possibilities

In the sky where dreams ignite,
Bright sparks dance through endless night.
Each shimmer holds a secret bright,
Guiding souls to futures light.

Across the waves, a whisper calls,
In every heart, potential sprawls.
With every step, our spirit soars,
To explore the vast open doors.

Hope paints trails on paths unknown,
As every thought can be our own.
With every choice, the future bends,
Toward horizons that never end.

So let us chase those shimmering lights,
Embrace the thrill of wondrous sights.
And in this journey, bold and free,
We'll write our own vast tapestry.

The Forgotten Stories of Twilight

When shadows stretch in evening's glow,
Whispers linger from long ago.
The tales of stars, the gentle night,
Hold echoes of forgotten flight.

Beneath the moon's soft silver tears,
Lies a world that stirs our fears.
Yet in the silence, hearts can see,
The beauty in old histories.

The twilight hosts a silent dance,
Of stories lost in fleeting chance.
Each shadow holds a secret tease,
Of loves and losses, tales that freeze.

So listen close as night unfolds,
For magic lies in voices old.
In twilight's charm, we find the way,
To worlds anew, where dreams can play.

Guardians of the Lost Knowledge

In the halls of faded lore,
Ancient whispers greet the floor.
Each book a key to dreams untold,
Guardians keep their secrets bold.

From depths of time, the wisdom calls,
In crumbling pages, the past enthralls.
With every word, the shadows lie,
Waiting for souls who dare to try.

The candle's flame reveals the path,
Through hidden tales and forgotten wrath.
In every lesson, spirits shine,
Knowledge flows through the hands of time.

So seek the truths that time has cast,
For in the knowledge, shadows last.
The guardians stand, their watch sincere,
To guide the hearts that choose to hear.

Reflections in the Starlit Abyss

In the darkness where stars align,
Reflections shimmer, pure and fine.
Each moment captured in deep space,
Holds remnants of a long-lost grace.

The void beyond, a canvas vast,
Where dreams are woven, futures cast.
In stillness, echoes softly play,
A symphony of night and day.

Within the abyss, our thoughts unite,
In silent whispers, we take flight.
Each glimmered hope, a guiding star,
Reveals a path, no matter how far.

So gaze into the cosmic flow,
And let your spirit freely go.
For in the depths, our truths await,
Reflections of our wondrous fate.

Horizons of the Mysterious

In twilight's glow, secrets dwell,
Whispers of winds begin to swell.
Mountains stand with tales untold,
Guardians of visions, brave and bold.

Stars awaken, a cosmic dance,
Framing shadows, lost in trance.
Rippling waters, paths obscure,
Calling forth the seekers, pure.

Fog-laden mornings unveil the dream,
With every heartbeat, silent scream.
Footsteps wander, never stray,
To find the dawn of a new day.

In the silence, echoes ring,
Each whisper holds a hidden spring.
Horizons beckon, journeys start,
With courage woven in each heart.

Layers of the Unrevealed

Veils of time in morning light,
Holding truths within their sight.
Beneath the surface, depths await,
Each layer drawn by fate's own weight.

Softly whispered, dreams unfold,
Stories linger, brave and bold.
Crimson skies with secrets share,
In every color, whispers flare.

River's current, ever strong,
Guides the lost to where they belong.
Rhythms pulse in hidden seams,
Woven threads of ancient dreams.

With every touch and every feel,
The heart discovers what is real.
Layers shift, a dance divine,
In the silence, stars align.

Crossroads of Curiosity

At intersections where paths divide,
Questions linger, hopes reside.
Eyes wide open, seeking light,
In every shadow, truths ignite.

Winds carry whispers of the unknown,
With every step, new seeds are sown.
With every choice, a road expands,
Crafting destinies with subtle hands.

In the heart of wonder's sway,
Choices beckon, lead the way.
A compass forged from dreams and fears,
Guides the way through shifting years.

Crossroads spark the flame of thought,
In every moment, lessons taught.
With open hearts we rise above,
Curiosity, the path of love.

Enveloping the Unexpressed

Silence wraps around the thought,
In hidden corners, courage fought.
Voices linger, yet unheard,
Echoes of dreams long deferred.

In shadows whisper, hopes concealed,
Gentle truth, yet unrevealed.
Colors vibrant in twilight's dream,
Painting feelings, lost in gleam.

Hearts beat softly, stories wait,
In every soul, a sealed fate.
Words unspoken, longing breath,
In the silence lies a depth.

Yet the night blooms with the stars,
Guiding seekers from afar.
In every heartbeat, silence pressed,
Awaits the dawn, the unexpressed.

Paths Untrodden

In the woods where silence thrives,
Whispers call from untraveled dives,
Echoes of dreams yet to explore,
Footsteps linger at life's door.

Beneath the boughs of ancient trees,
Breath of solace in the breeze,
Each step taken, a choice to make,
A journey born from paths we take.

Lost in thoughts, the mind can roam,
Seeking solace far from home,
In the stillness, shadows play,
Guiding hearts to find their way.

With every turn, new tales arise,
Unseen worlds beneath the skies,
In the dance of light and shade,
Brave the paths where dreams are made.

Veils of Enigma

In shadows cast by cryptic night,
Mysteries hide, avoiding sight,
Whispers linger, secrets curl,
Threads of fate in muted swirl.

Behind the gaze of tranquil eyes,
Veils conceal the silent cries,
Stories untold in hidden smiles,
Echoing softly through the miles.

Time flows softly, a gentle hand,
Guiding souls through an unseen land,
Like echoes fading in the mist,
The secrets yearn to be unkissed.

In puzzles deep, the heart must delve,
Finding pieces within oneself,
For in the heart, the truth may bloom,
Even veils may fade in light of noon.

Shadows of Forgotten Truths

In corners dim where memories lie,
Shadows whisper, time goes by,
Echoes of laughter, hints of woe,
Dancing softly in the glow.

Once vibrant tales, now dressed in dust,
Buried beneath, we learn to trust,
In faded ink and tarnished gold,
The warmth of stories yet untold.

As time unwinds its tangled thread,
Forgotten voices fill the dread,
Yet hope arises from old dreams,
Beneath the surface, nothing seems.

For shadows hold the lightiest truths,
Where silence guards our driven youths,
In silent corners, hearts will see,
The past entwined with mystery.

Luminance in the Dark

When night descends and hope seems lost,
Stars above remind us of the cost,
For in the void, a spark takes flight,
Illuminating paths with gentle light.

Each flicker dances, wild and free,
Whispering dreams for you and me,
Guiding journeys with beams so bright,
Leading souls through the endless night.

In darkness deep, resilience glows,
Through trials faced, true spirit shows,
A tapestry of strength is sewn,
With luminous threads, we are never alone.

So when you wander, lost and stark,
Remember the flame that ignites the dark,
For in the shadows, beauty's found,
In every heartbeat, love surrounds.

The Invisible Thread We Weave

In twilight's glow, we softly tread,
Binding dreams with words unsaid.
Through whispers sweet, our spirits dance,
Entangled hearts, a fleeting glance.

Beneath the stars, our secrets fly,
In quiet nights, where echoes lie.
With every thread, our lives entwine,
A tapestry, both yours and mine.

In laughter shared, in sorrows borne,
Through silent storms, or quiet morn.
Each fragile strand, a bond we hold,
Stories written, in love retold.

As seasons turn, the threads may fray,
Yet in our hearts, they'll always stay.
Connected still, we strive to see,
The invisible thread that sets us free.

Murmurs from Beneath the Surface

Beneath the waves, where silence dwells,
Soft murmurs rise, like distant bells.
Secrets held in liquid blue,
Whispers echo, deep and true.

The tide reveals what shadows hide,
In fleeting glimpses, worlds collide.
Ebb and flow, a timeless game,
Carried forth by currents' name.

In depths unknown, life's pulse is found,
Nature's voice, a sacred sound.
Glimmers dance on water's skin,
Inviting hearts to dive within.

With every wave, new tales unfold,
Mysteries of the deep retold.
In ocean's heart, our dreams entwine,
Murmurs soft, like aged wine.

The Enigma Wrapped in Silence

In shadows cast by moonlit sheen,
Lies the truth, so often unseen.
Wrapped in silence, a story waits,
Unraveling slowly at time's fates.

Whispers linger in the night air,
Hints of secrets, a silent prayer.
In stillness profound, we seek to find,
The enigma veiled, forever blind.

Words unspoken, yet loudly felt,
With every glance, the mystery dealt.
A glance exchanged, a moment shared,
The heart reveals what's never bared.

In quietude, the truth will bloom,
In silence, echoes dispel the gloom.
A riddle wrapped in layers deep,
Awaits the souls who dare to leap.

Footprints in the Veiled Garden

In twilight's grace, the garden sighs,
Footprints trace where memory lies.
Petals fall like whispers sweet,
Marking paths of love's retreat.

Through softest shades, the shadows creep,
Where secrets held in silence sleep.
Amongst the blooms, we seek to roam,
Finding solace, finding home.

The fragrant breeze shares tales of old,
Of joys embraced and sorrows told.
Each footprint left, a story spun,
In veils of green, we become one.

As moonlight bathes the world in white,
Our hearts align, in shared delight.
In veiled gardens, love remains,
A timeless bond that never wanes.

Fragments of the Unrevealed

Shadows whisper secrets untold,
In corners where truths dare not unfold.
Time holds fragments, broken and strange,
Lost in the silence of fear and change.

Eyes stare deeply, searching the maze,
For glimmers of light in the hazy haze.
Each breath a question, each sigh a call,
In fragments scattered, we rise and fall.

Moments suspended, poised on the brink,
As echoes of memory beckon to think.
We gather the pieces, we yearn to see,
The beauty concealed in what cannot be.

With every heartbeat, a story is spun,
In shadows and light, the dance has begun.
Embrace the unseen, reveal what's concealed,
For life's deepest truths are often unhealed.

Threads of the Unspoken

Between the words that linger and sigh,
Are threads of silence that flutter and fly.
Weave them together, a tapestry grand,
Of dreams left unsaid, like grains of sand.

In hushed tones, a melody flows,
With unspoken tales that nobody knows.
Each heartbeat a whisper, a longing in gray,
Unraveled by moments, lost in the fray.

Glimpse of connections that never are formed,
In the quietest corners where feelings are warmed.
A hush that encircles, a bond that is real,
In threads of the unspoken, our hearts gently feel.

So listen intently, to pauses and sighs,
In silence resides the truth behind eyes.
For in the unvoiced, our spirits entwine,
With threads of the unspoken, forever divine.

Riddles in the Fog

Thick as a veil, the fog blankets all,
With riddles entwined, in whispers they call.
Step into shadows, let realms intertwine,
Where visions collide, and mysteries shine.

Fog wraps the world in a tender embrace,
Shrouded in wonder, we traverse space.
A puzzle of silence, where nothing seems clear,
Each moment a riddle, a dance sincere.

Echoes of laughter, faint in the mist,
Threads of the past that beckon, persist.
What lies beyond? What secrets are hid?
In riddles of fog, we ponder and bid.

So wander the pathways where shadows reside,
In riddles of fog, let your heart be your guide.
Embrace the unknown, let the enigma unfold,
For beauty is born in the tales left untold.

The Palette of Concealment

Colors that blend, yet never reveal,
Painted in layers, a canvas surreal.
The palette of concealment, rich and profound,
Hides stories and secrets, waiting to be found.

Brush strokes of silence, a delicate touch,
Crafting a vision that says far too much.
Each hue a memory, each shade a sigh,
In the art of concealment, the heart learns to fly.

Splashes of laughter, shadows of tears,
Canvas of moments, painted with fears.
In every corner, a truth intertwined,
The palette of concealment, a story defined.

So gaze at the artwork, let intuition guide,
For in shades of the hidden, our souls can abide.
Embrace the colors that whisper and speak,
In the palette of concealment, we find what we seek.

Voyages into the Unexplored

Sailing on the whispers of the night,
Hidden realms awaken from their flight.
Stars align to guide the daring hearts,
As dreams unfurl, a quest that never parts.

Lost in mist where shadows intertwine,
Each wave holds secrets, ancient and divine.
The compass sways, yet courage finds its way,
Into the vast unknown, we boldly sway.

Wonders wait in every distant shore,
The promise of adventure we adore.
With every tale, the horizon lifts its veil,
In untamed lands, we craft our own fairytale.

Footprints fade on sands of time's embrace,
Yet memories linger, we leave our trace.
To voyages unknown, let our spirits soar,
In the unexplored, forever yearning for more.

Folding into Shadows

In twilight's glow, where secrets softly creep,
Shadows dance, in silence, they will leap.
The world shifts, a tapestry of night,
Folding whispers into the heart's delight.

Beneath the veil, where echoes softly sing,
Every glance reveals a hidden thing.
The past unfolds, like parchment worn and frayed,
In these shadows, all is not dismayed.

Silence cradles stories left untold,
In darkness, truths and mysteries unfold.
Each moment bends, a flicker in the dark,
Folding deep into shadows, we embark.

What lies beneath the surface of the known,
In shadows, secrets shimmer and are grown.
So let us fold, immerse in night's embrace,
Finding light in shadows, a sacred space.

Crafts of the Concealed

In hidden nooks where dreams are spun like thread,
Crafts of the concealed, where few have dared to tread.
Hands skilled in whispers, weaving tales anew,
In every stitch, a story waits for you.

Secrets buried in layers, rich and deep,
Craftsmen of the shadows, their vigil they keep.
With every breath, an essence brought to life,
In the quiet corners, creativity rife.

Textures speak in a language soft and clear,
Crafted with passion, intentions sincere.
What is unseen can shape the world we know,
In the crafts concealed, the spirit's glow.

Revealing treasures hidden from plain sight,
Creating beauty in the depth of night.
Let us celebrate the art of what we find,
In crafts of the concealed, we intertwine.

Illusions of Clarity

Mirrors reflect what the heart yearns to see,
Illusions of clarity, a tender decree.
In the gaze of a dream, the truth may bend,
Yet through the chaos, we find our end.

Glimmers of insight flicker like a flame,
In the pursuit of wisdom, none are the same.
What seems so clear may be shrouded in mist,
Yet we chase the outlines of a fleeting tryst.

A serenade of thoughts, softly they weave,
Illusions dance, but reality can grieve.
Hold on to the doubts that curl like smoke,
In seeking clarity, a new path is woke.

Trust the journey, let the shadows play,
In the heart of the storm, clarity may sway.
For in illusions, we often find a guide,
Leading us onward, with dreams as our stride.

The Uncharted Depths Await

In shadows deep where silence dwells,
Secrets whisper, time repels.
A heart that dares to dive so far,
Finds treasures lost, a guiding star.

Waves may crash and storms may roar,
Yet brave souls seek what's on the shore.
The tides of fate will ebb and flow,
Charting paths that few will know.

With every plunge into the night,
New worlds unfold, revealing light.
The depths, once dark, now gleam with grace,
Adventure waits in this vast space.

So heed the call of ocean's song,
For in the depths, you will belong.
Embrace the unknown, let it ignite,
A journey forged from dreams in flight.

Gates of the Unrevealed Mysteries

At twilight's edge, where shadows blend,
A portal rests, where pathways bend.
Each door, adorned with tales untold,
Invites the brave, both young and old.

With every step, the heart will race,
Through whispers soft in hidden space.
Secrets wrapped in twilight's glow,
Awaiting souls willing to know.

The locks of fate shall yield with trust,
In every dream, in every gust.
Open the gates, let wonders spill,
Unravel the threads of fate's great will.

So dare to cross the threshold wide,
Where every mystery will abide.
In realms unknown, we weave our fate,
At gates of awe, we celebrate.

Beyond the Horizon of Dreams

Where sky meets earth in hues so bright,
Beyond the horizon, the heart takes flight.
Dreams like waves, they rise and fall,
Calling the brave to heed their call.

In realms unseen, where visions sway,
Awaits a path, a vibrant way.
With every heartbeat, fate will steer,
Infusing life with magic dear.

The stars embrace the dusk's soft light,
Whispering secrets of the night.
Beyond the bounds of time and space,
Endless possibilities grace.

So journey forth, let courage bloom,
In dreams that banish darkest gloom.
For on the horizon, joy awaits,
Beyond the threshold, open gates.

Constellations of the Unspoken

In silent skies, where starlight sings,
Lie tales of love and hidden things.
Constellations weave their endless lore,
In the hush of night, they softly pour.

Each twinkling light, a thought concealed,
Whispers of souls that time has healed.
The bonds we share, though rarely voiced,
In nightly dance, our hearts rejoiced.

Among the stars, dreams take their flight,
Illuminating paths in the night.
With every glance, a story shared,
In constellations, souls are bared.

So heed the silence, listen close,
For in the quiet, love will rose.
In unspoken words, our spirits find,
A universe where hearts are aligned.

Arcane Reveries

In shadows deep where secrets lie,
Whispers of old softly sigh.
Lost in the twilight's gentle hold,
Mysteries weave, tales untold.

Ancient echoes call my name,
A dance of thoughts, wild and tame.
Fragments of dreams, vivid and bright,
Guide my heart through the night.

Patterns unseen | within the dark,
Flicker like stars, a hesitant spark.
In the stillness, magic flows,
Arcane reveries gently grow.

Unraveling threads of fate's design,
Each woven stitch, a sign divine.
Through time's embrace, I shall roam,
In this vast realm, I find my home.

Beyond the Obscured

Veils of mist drape the dawn,
Yet beauty lies where light is drawn.
With each step, the world transforms,
Past the shadows, new life warms.

Secrets linger in the air,
Chasing echoes, none compare.
Over hills where dreams entwine,
Whispers beckon, a soft sign.

Wander far where visions stir,
Faith in sights that gently blur.
Beyond the obscured, hope awaits,
Invitation to the fates.

Eyes wide open, hearts set free,
In this realm, we come to be.
Through the haze, we journey forth,
To rich terrains of boundless worth.

The Language of Silence

In the quiet, thoughts take flight,
Whispered dreams ignite the night.
A stillness deep, a world within,
Where echoes of truth softly spin.

Echoes dance on a breath's sigh,
Voices unheard, yet none deny.
In silence, hearts begin to see,
The language speaks, wild and free.

Feel the pulse of unspoken grace,
In every moment, time and space.
Guardians of all that we fear,
The language of silence draws us near.

Listen close, the secrets unfold,
Stories cherished, ancient and bold.
In hushed tones, the world ignites,
A chorus of stars on the endless nights.

Portals of Discovery

Glimmers of light, hidden doors,
Paths through the silence, endless shores.
With every step, a tale unfurls,
In the tapestry of countless worlds.

Portals call from valleys deep,
Awakening dreams long asleep.
Through every threshold, wisdom flows,
In the embrace of what life knows.

Fragments of time, woven thread,
Whispers of places we've never tread.
Adventures unfold, bold and bright,
Under the cover of starlit night.

Seek the wonders that lie ahead,
In each encounter, let hope be fed.
For beyond the known, magic waits,
In the portals of discovery, open the gates.

Constellations of Hidden Thoughts

Amidst the vast and silent night,
Stars echo dreams that take their flight.
Whispers dance on cosmic waves,
In shadows deep, our secret caves.

Each twinkling light a thought concealed,
Silent prayers that time revealed.
Galaxies spin, in quiet thrall,
Mapping paths where shadows fall.

In twilight's gaze, we search for signs,
Drifting through the tangled lines.
Connections lost, yet softly found,
In starlit realms, our hearts unbound.

Hidden truths in twilight gleam,
Woven softly in a dream.
Constellations whisper low,
Guiding us where we must go.

The Backdrop of Silence

In stillness, whispers cradle time,
Each moment held, a fleeting rhyme.
The world slows down, a tranquil breath,
As silence weaves its subtle depth.

Beneath the weight of night's embrace,
Thoughts unravel, find their place.
Shadows flicker, dance and fade,
In quietude, our fears are laid.

The universe learns to listen close,
To hearts that beat, as stillness grows.
In absence loud, we find our voice,
A deeper calm, a kinder choice.

The backdrop soft, a canvas wide,
In silence, all our truths abide.
With every heartbeat, every sigh,
We craft our tales beneath the sky.

Whims of the Unseen

In shadows soft, where echoes play,
The unseen guides us on our way.
A breeze that whispers, tales untold,
In fleeting moments, secrets unfold.

The dance of leaves, a silent muse,
A symphony in every hue.
Whims of fate in gentle touch,
Remind us that we're all but much.

Stars align in patterns rare,
While dreams take flight on wings of air.
In every heartbeat, every glance,
The unseen weaves its subtle dance.

So let us wander, hearts unchained,
Embrace the whims that life has gained.
For in the dark, there shines a spark,
A guiding light within the dark.

Secrets Written in the Stars

Above us lie the ancient tales,
Stories woven in cosmic sails.
Each star a word, each constellation,
Holds the dreams of every nation.

Secrets hidden in the night,
Waiting for the wise to write.
In celestial ink, fate is penned,
A journey started, never ends.

We gaze above, our hopes align,
Seeking truth in spaces divine.
Galactic whispers call our name,
Within the stars, we play the game.

So let our spirits reach the sky,
In every constellation, why?
For in this vast and timeless sea,
Lie the secrets of you and me.

Uncharted Echoes

In the silent woods they call,
Whispers dance where shadows fall.
Footsteps lead to dreams untold,
Secrets buried, hearts of gold.

Beneath the stars, a path unfolds,
Guided by the night so bold.
Every rustle, every sigh,
Marks the echoes drifting by.

Hidden realms that time forgot,
In their depths, a sacred plot.
Voices linger on the breeze,
In this place, the spirit's ease.

Adventure waits in muted tones,
Where every heart claims its own throngs.
So follow where the wild winds blow,
And find the truth in shadows' glow.

Mysteries in Twilight

When daylight fades to dusky hues,
The world wraps in a gentle muse.
Stars ignite with stories old,
In the twilight's embrace, secrets unfold.

Night unfurls its silken wing,
Softly humming what dreams may bring.
Figures dance in fading light,
Whispers soft as the approaching night.

Shadows stretch and mingle near,
Carrying hopes, unraveling fear.
In the stillness, magic weaves,
Entwined in tales that night believes.

So pause and breathe the evening air,
Let go of worries, shed despair.
For in the dark, the wonders play,
Awakening truths in the heart's ballet.

Unveiling the Veil

Behind the veil, the wonders gleam,
Mystical threads of a vivid dream.
Each layer whispers, beckons close,
Revealing what the heart must choose.

With every tear, a glimpse bestowed,
Of magic paths and stories flowed.
What lies beneath, a heart's desire,
Awakening the latent fire.

We shed the doubts, we cast aside,
And walk the path where dreams abide.
In trembling moments, truth is found,
In the silence, a love profound.

So lift the veil and feel its grace,
In hidden corners, find your place.
For life's enchantment waits in store,
With every heartbeat, seek for more.

Enigmatic Horizons

Beyond the reach of sight and sound,
Where shadows play on hollow ground.
Horizons call with mysteries rare,
Inviting hearts to wander, dare.

In the distance, colors blend,
Crafting tales that seem to bend.
Every sunrise paints the skies,
Inspiring dreams where hope can rise.

The echoes of the past remain,
Guide the lost through joy and pain.
In fleeting moments, wisdom grows,
As the heart reaches where love flows.

So venture forth to where you yearn,
And let the fire of life brightly burn.
For every step unveils a chance,
To dance along the grand expanse.

Whispers in the Twilight

The sun dips low, the sky aglow,
A breeze caresses with secrets known.
Stars awaken, flickering bright,
Whispers dance in the fading light.

Shadows lengthen, the world stands still,
Crickets serenade the night's chill thrill.
Moonbeams herald a silver song,
In twilight's grip, where dreams belong.

The trees sway gently, lost in thought,
Their voices soft, in silence caught.
As dusk envelops, time slips away,
In twilight's arms, forever to stay.

A moment held, a sigh released,
In whispered tales, our hearts find peace.
Together in twilight, we find our way,
Embraced by night, where shadows play.

Chronicles of the Unfathomed

Beneath the waves, where silence lies,
Mysteries sleep beneath dark skies.
Ancient tales in currents weave,
Chronicles held, waiting to leave.

Ghostly ships in the depths roam,
Carrying whispers of long-lost home.
The depths conceal what eyes can't see,
An ocean's heart, wild and free.

Secrets wrapped in watery lace,
A kingdom thriving in hidden space.
The sirens sing to lure the bold,
Unfathomed truths waiting to unfold.

In tidal waves and gentle tides,
The ocean's lore forever resides.
A world apart, yet close at hand,
In the deep embrace of shifting sand.

A Tapestry of Shadows

In twilight's weave, shadows entwine,
Colors blend, both soft and fine.
Each thread a story, each hue a sigh,
A tapestry spun as time slips by.

Echoes linger in the woven ground,
In patterns rich, our dreams are found.
Between the light and dark we tread,
Crafting futures from words unsaid.

Textures whisper, secrets unfold,
As ancient tales are softly told.
In every fold, a memory glows,
In shadows cast, true beauty shows.

This tapestry holds all we've shared,
Love and loss, the lives we dared.
Together we weave, through joy and pain,
A work of art that shall remain.

Underneath the Stillness

Beneath the calm, a heartbeat stirs,
Where quiet lingers, life occurs.
In silent moments, we find our place,
A hidden world, a sacred space.

The air is thick with thoughts unsaid,
In shadows whispering, secrets spread.
Time ebbs gently, a flowing stream,
In stillness, we breathe, we dream.

The stars are hushed, the moon a guide,
In quietude, we oft confide.
What lies beneath the surface still,
Is echoed softly within our will.

So here we pause, beneath the night,
In stillness wrapped, we find the light.
With every breath, a story grows,
Underneath stillness, our spirit flows.

Light Shy of Disclosure

In shadows we find whispered dreams,
Flickers of truth, not what they seem.
A veil of silence drapes the night,
Hiding the glimmers, dimming the light.

Secrets lie in the depths of eyes,
Beneath the surface, the heart denies.
Rumors dance like flickering flames,
An echo of hope that softly claims.

What is hidden struggles to glow,
Yet in the silence, the yearnings flow.
Each murmur carries a tender song,
In the absence of light, we still belong.

But still we linger on paths unclear,
Chasing the shadows, holding them near.
For though the truth may choose to hide,
The soul's desire can never abide.

Remains of the Hidden

In forgotten corners, stories rest,
Silent echoes of all that's best.
A tapestry woven with threads of time,
Hiding the peaks of truth's steep climb.

The echoes whisper from walls so thick,
Time wears away with a gentle tick.
Lost in pages of ancient lore,
Wanderers seek what once was more.

Between the lines of faded prose,
A hint of fate and the tale it chose.
Bits of the past in shadows concealed,\nOffer the heart a chance to be healed.

But here we stand, on the edge of light,
Hoping to grasp the heights of insight.
What remains hidden will one day show,
The beauty of life that we long to know.

Allure of the Unseen

In the depths of dusk, the mysteries call,
Drawn to the allure, we dare to fall.
Veils of desire weave through the night,
Glimmers of dreams flicker, ignite.

The unseen touches with gentle grace,
A brush of shadows, a fleeting trace.
Every heartbeat sings a hidden tune,
Echoing softly beneath the moon.

What we can't grasp, we long to hold,
In the silence, stories unfold.
Eyes closed tight, yet we feel the spark,
The allure of secrets hidden in the dark.

Always we search for that subtle sign,
To guide our way, as stars align.
For in the unseen, beauty does bloom,
A dance of life shrouded in gloom.

Streams of Intrigue

Along the waters, secrets flow,
Currents shift, in whispers low.
Hidden tales in the ripples glide,
Mirroring dreams that we confide.

Each twist and turn holds a surprise,
Reflections murmur beneath the skies.
A journey woven with threads of chance,
Where shadows invite us to dance.

Waves of stories, old and new,
Carried softly, like morning dew.
From banks unknown, the past unfurls,
Revealing the magic of hidden worlds.

In the stream's embrace, we find our way,
Guided by echoes of yesterday.
With every flow, intrigue persists,
Fueling our hearts with gentle twists.

Milton Keynes UK
Ingram Content Group UK Ltd.
UKHW021937121124
451129UK00007B/124

9 789916 889763